RODNEY J. HILL

Web Copywriting Fundamentals

Contents

1

Introduction

"How do you find the right words?".

This is THE question that any writer should ask themselves before sitting down at the pc and putting their hand to the keyboard.

Depending on what our audience is, we will have to adapt our writing style and depending on what our goal is, we will have to adapt the way we write.

Remember: you can have some difficulties when writing something that will potentially be read by a multitude of people.

I have personally realized this, managing for over 5 years a Facebook page with over 200,000 followers linked to a satirical project of mine (Honest Dinosaurs).

Before publishing, I take a deep breath and check the content of the post at least three times. Yes, because when we write online we hardly imagine that the text is physically read by someone. And yet it is so: the funny posts I publish have a user base that corresponds to the number of spectators in the San Siro stadium at a Vasco Rossi concert or an Inter-Juventus match. Multiplied by three!

To begin with, let's keep in mind that the basic elements of good writing remain the same.

You must choose the right words and vocabulary suitable for what is the communicative objective, which you must predetermine even before you start writing.

Also, using correct grammar is definitely one of the most important features to keep in mind when writing.

Also very important is punctuation, which I have found to be one of the biggest problems for those who want to start writing.

Before you start thinking about writing for work study very well when to put a period, when to put a comma, how to insert a quote or a quotation mark, how to use a semicolon.

I know, these are the basics, but all of this is not so obvious.

To conclude the list of indispensable notions that every web copywriter should have, clearly, I would put the emphasis on what concerns syntax, that is, the ability to process elements and put them in a sequence that leads to the greatest and best possible effect.

This book is dedicated to all those who want to approach writing for the web.

INTRODUCTION

We're going to learn how to structure a text, what are the differences between traditional and online writing and many techniques to make our articles more effective.

Good reading

2

The challenges of online writing

Attention Threshold

The most important thing a web copywriter should keep in mind is the attention threshold of their audience.

When we're reading a book, e-book on our tablet or a print article we're usually completely isolated. On the other hand, if we're nibbling on an article on a smartphone, which is tiny and doesn't have the size of the book, and maybe we're on the subway or walking around, we'll soon realize that the attention span is absolutely low.

The context of traditional reading is quiet and relaxed, while the context of online reading is hectic.

The key word is distraction

It also depends on the device on which we read: the traditional book is something physical that we hold in our hands and it's big enough to deserve our full attention. On the web, things change, and quite a bit.

We must therefore ask ourselves what online users are looking for through reading, which despite the spread of image and video based social networks (Instagram, TikTok, Youtube) maintains a role of absolute prestige in the fruition of multimedia content via the Internet.

Web users are looking for immediate gratification: no waiting, no effort, just a click to enter a whole new world full of information.

Cannibals in search of information

Here is the motto of online users: "give me everything right away, give it to me in the first lines".

So, let's remember that one of the characteristics of online writing is immediacy.

To get read online we must learn the ancient art of synthesis, put the main information in the first few lines and do a great job on the headline.

There are no real readers anymore when we talk about online reading. We can call them more of users, because it radically changes the way we read and digest information.

Quoting the greatest usability expert for the web, Jakob Nielsen:

"Users are no longer reading, but rather taking advantage of exploratory reading."

Let's look at that for a moment.

When we explore online we read two lines of an article, click on a link and read three more lines, then we look at a photo, go back to Facebook, read a post, etc..

This is precisely why we can call it exploratory reading.

Users are used to immediacy

And this is where SEO writing comes into play, namely all those techniques that serve to position our articles, our texts on search engines, to ensure that users find in them a relevant answer to their question.

Because that's exactly what users are looking for: answers.

Fast, relevant and concise answers

Just imagine any search, which we can perform on any engine such as Google, to realize that we don't have time to waste and we go to click on the most immediate and consistent result in relation to our question.

Screen factor

To understand how complex it is to read texts online we must also consider the "screen factor".

We just said it, reading on screen is a more difficult reading, a bit more arcane, everything is smaller and more confusing.

There are hypertext links, so the user goes "jumping" from one web page to another (which is the very basis of hypertextuality). We are no longer talking about vertical reading from beginning to end, but a protean type of reading, so our online experience is based on branching.

Think of the example of Wikipedia: you go to a Wikipedia page, then each keyword leads to another entry, so maybe you don't even finish reading the full text but jump from one page to another to go deeper.

Exploratory reading

In short, we can say that 80%, if not almost 100%, of online users do not go beyond the first paragraph.

I say 80% because maybe the first paragraph is a bit long, but if it's pretty short basically everyone reads it.

After that, the second paragraph will surely be read by a smaller percentage, 70-60%, and so on: few reach the end.

So you must, or should, take this factor into account and try to place all the crucial information in the first paragraph that can then act as a lever to keep people reading.

Conceptual and visual hooks

In online writing we basically have to put conceptual and visual hooks to guide (and keep) the reader, while in traditional writing there is no such problem: if I write a novel I don't have to put everything in the first paragraph!

When writing a blog article, for example, it's important to capture the user's attention with the title and the first paragraph. Because that's what he wants: to figure out as quickly as possible if that content is for him.

As you go down with the reading (eh yes, because this is the "scrolling" reading mode on smartphones) more and more people will abandon, so we must try to put all the crucial information at the top of the text.

Clearly, it's also important to work on the headline, which is the reason why people go to click and read an article.

So, remember that the top part of the text is definitely the section you need to take into consideration the most when you are in the difficult and hectic environment of online writing.

Interactivity

We said that one of the peculiar features of online reading is interactivity.

Users can decide the path, the maze to follow, which is different for each of them.

In addition to this, we must take into account that there are other multimedia contents that usually accompany our article.

There are also music, photographs, videos, internal links and external links to our article and related content.

Distraction can be considered the order of the day.

Brevity

Online writing must be concise and pragmatic.

"Pragmatic" in the sense that, without too many turns of phrase, you should go and place at the top of the article or post, and even better in the title, what is the juiciest information that could to some extent go to satisfy the reader's need (we will see later how this is the most used strategy online, but certainly not the only one).

Summarizing

To recap, the challenges of online writing are:

1. Attention span
2. Immediate gratification
3. The screen factor, hence the difficulty of reading online on tablets, PCs and smartphones.
4. The fact that there are no longer real readers, but cannibals who seek to satisfy their hunger for information in an absolutely immediate way.
5. Then there are the challenges of interactivity and writing for search engines.

3

SEO Copywriting

How a Search Engine Works

How does a search engine work and why is it important to know how to write keeping in mind how it works?

Perhaps not everyone knows that a search engine is a software that indexes all the text on the web according to its relevance.

The most famous one and the one we all use every day is surely Google, but there are also others such as, for example, Bing by Microsoft or DuckDuckGo (the search engine that cares about your privacy, I highly recommend it as an alternative to Google).

Virtual spiders

Search engines send daily crawlers or spiders, virtual spiders, to scan and read all the pages of the web (which in English means precisely "spider's web").

These spiders go to Google's headquarters to report all the information, trying to understand what the text is about: is it an article about organic fruit rather than an article about a new perfume?

Spiders are constantly traveling, day in and day out, scanning, reading and reporting information.

This justifies the fact that if you publish an article it will take a few hours before it appears on search engines: let's say that spiders are like Santa Claus... They visit everyone, but it takes at least one night!

As all the information is collected within the database, it is ranked, so we talk about ranking or ranking of online texts based on certain search keys.

Relevant Solutions

The reasoning behind the search engine is the following: when the user searches for X I will show all the solutions relevant to X in an increasing ranking from the most suitable to the least suitable.

Obviously the principle at the base of the search engine is that of pertinence.

Let's understand a moment what is the relevance: "relevance" means trivially the best answer for the query, for the question that the user asks.

If the user asks a question, the search engine, depending on the ranking and the importance and the score that is given for example to your article, will show you in first position, second position or fifth position.

A competitive context

We are in a competitive type of context, because if I publish on my blog an article about the best apps for traveling, there will be hundreds of other authors who have already written an article of this type.

So, how can we try to climb this ranking and appear with this article in the top positions?

Let's say right now that there is no magic wand (and that the tricks you find online leave time to find), but I can tell you to go first to structure the text through html tags, "labels", which you should know if you write texts online.

Optimize html

In the html code, which is the language that underlies online communication, we have the h tags, which stands for heading, ranging from h1 to h6.

The element marked with h1 is basically the main title and the search engine understands this and takes it as a reference.

The tags are basically suggestions that we give to the search engines. The h2 will be the subtitle, then we have the tag p which stands for paragraph, used precisely for paragraphs.

But how do we elaborate an article at technical html level?

A standard article has a single h1, that is a main title, an h2 with the value of subtitle and, depending on the length of the text, some h3 that can go to titrate the various paragraphs (which are marked by the tag p).

All this is useful for the search engine to understand the structure of the article, to try to index it in the best way and to understand the internal scaffolding of your text.

Generally speaking, the title is more important than the subtitle. For this reason, even visually an h1 will be written in larger fonts than an h2 or h3.

You need to start thinking about your content in a hierarchical order, precisely because that's how Google thinks.

Also, bold words are an indicator of importance to spiders.

So it's ok to work first on the quality of your title, on the textual, syntactic, grammatical and lexical quality, but remember to always go to mark the elements with these labels, which will allow the search engine to read more fluently the content and to index better what is your work.

Summing up

You have to learn how to structure the text at html (hyper text markup language) level, which in a nutshell is a set of tags, labels that surround the various elements to explain to the search engine or to the browser what is the structure and content of your article.

The difficulty is twofold: there is the question of the quality of the text, but there is also that of going to subdivide it into various sections in a structured and intelligent way.

4

Keywords

Short head and long tail

When we talk about keywords to insert in an article for the web we must immediately make a technical distinction.

There are two main types of keywords: short head and long tail.

What is the difference?

Let's assume that we are writing an article about Christmas vacations in New York in which we will need to insert keywords to allow the search engine to do its job.

Let's write our fascinating and engaging headline, perhaps with a question, such as "Do you know this year's top 10 destinations? Discover New York" or "Discover New York in the snow. An offer not to be missed."

In the body copy (the substantial part of the article) we are going to insert in a natural way some keywords such as: 'Christmas vacations in New York', 'vacations in New York', 'Christmas in New York'.

Short heads are rather short keywords. Be careful though, the keyword is not represented by the single word but by the single concept.

For example, 'vacation in New York' is a unique keyword and is a short head keyword.

However, being a very short and not very specific keyword, the competition we will have with other websites using the same keyword will be very high.

For this reason we often use the famous technique of long tail keywords, which are much broader and longer concepts that guarantee less competition.

For example, if I enter "Christmas vacation in New York with a visit to the Empire State Building", this is a long tail keyword. It represents a more refined concept, a highly specific user search (not only do they want to spend Christmas in New York but they also have an urge to visit the famous skyscraper).

But let's go into more detail.

We have seen a short keyword and a much longer one and we have said that in the first example the number of online competitors that will talk about the same subject will be much larger, consequently it will be very difficult to rank well with that keyword.

Instead, if you use the longer keyword surely there will be many less websites mentioning and using this keyword, so it will be much easier to rank in search in the first pages of Google.

In fact, if you enter a more specific query you will find fewer results than if you enter a more generic one.

The skill of the web copywriter and those who want to write for the web is to try to go and use long-tail keywords and shorter keywords to create a harmony that allows the search engine to understand what you are talking about.

So I suggest you do this: when you want to make an article make two circles on a sheet of paper, one circle "shorter keywords" and one circle "long keywords".

Then select three to five in the first and three to five in the second.

This will allow you to have a focus and put the most relevant and intelligent keywords within your article.

You will then be writing a fantastic article while keeping in mind all the little rules of good keyword usage that the web requires.

Keyword stuffing

A piece of advice that I would like to give you is to avoid like the plague what in technical jargon is called keyword stuffing, that is that technique (obsolete and penalizing) that consists in filling the article with keywords just to climb in the search engines.

I know, the temptation is great but trust me: stuffing the article with dozens of keywords is never a good idea and is counterproductive.

The use of keywords should be sensible and relevant, so when you enter a keyword ask yourself: does it make sense to put it in or am I just doing it for the search engines?

If the answer is the latter, you might not want to put it in.

As said, keyword stuffing is a technique that Google penalizes and that risks to relegate your article (or domain) in the Internet oblivion.

5

The lineup and pre-writing phase

Thinking, writing and correcting

What I'm proposing is a tripartite model, with a prewriting phase, a free writing phase and a rewriting phase. In Italian: think, write and correct. A scheme that you can certainly adapt to your needs.

It serves to make a bit 'of clarity on how to develop texts for the web, but also for the printed paper or the writing of larger texts, such as short stories and novels.

Article design phase

The first phase of the three is called prewriting and it is a phase during which we will think and design what we want to go write.

We're going to brainstorm and identify the focus and keywords to be included and then draft an outline.

Right now, we haven't written a line of our article yet, but we're simply trying to work and reason so that we can have an easier time in the later stages.

The outline is absolutely necessary, because it establishes the structure of your text and determines its internal logic.

One of the biggest mistakes people make when writing is not planning and skipping this prewriting stage.

How do I come up with an outline?

My method (which I recommend) is to choose the topic we want to talk about and make a list of, approximately, 5 items. These 5 headings represent the various digressions/declinations of the main topic (don't worry, later on we'll see how to generate creative ideas for our articles).

Only after elaborating on these topics do I go on to write an introduction and a conclusion.

The standard structure is this

ARGUMENT

- Introduction

- Theme 1
- Theme 2
- Theme 3
- Theme 4
- Theme 5
- Conclusions

Let's take a clarifying example.

I want to write an article about Wordpress and why it is smart to use it to make websites. In the first point I'm going to put maybe an introduction to Wordpress, in the second point I can put some successful case studies of people who have used it, in point three the advantages of using it, in point four the alternatives to Wordpress and in point five why Wordpress is the best of these systems.

Once I have this lineup of five drawn up, I'm going to add an introduction and a conclusion.

In the conclusion I will definitely include a call to action, a type of phrase (marked by the imperative verbal mode, i.e. a real command) that is used a lot in social media and online, such as "if you liked the article leave a comment" or "what do you think? Write it in the comments."

Here's our full lineup:

- Introduction
- What is Wordpress
- Case Studies

- Benefits of use
- Alternatives to Wordpress
- Why it is the best choice
- Conclusions
- CTA

At this stage of prewriting, we were able to easily get the skeleton of the article (which is practically already written).

Obviously each of these five points, depending on the complexity of our article, can be extended.

6

The first draft

Start writing

Once you have selected these 5 (or more, at your discretion) micro-sections we can move on to the free writing phase, which will consist of "populating", filling in these five blocks to which I have practically already given a title.

Well, maybe you didn't realize it, but elaborating the skeleton of the article in this way you will not only have a structure that guarantees an internal logic, but you will also have the ideas for the titles of your "sections".

Of course, a revision will be necessary, but in this way you have associated each section with a concept and it will be impossible to go off-topic or waste time on long dissertations that are inconsistent with your chosen topic.

Free writing

In the freewriting phase you can write your text without worrying too much about grammar or syntax. Write, improvise, don't think about it: there is always time to revise.

Unravel the themes of the blocks, and make sure that all 5 have a consistent length between them. At this stage you can move from one block to another: as soon as you have an idea, add it.

More advanced text structures have additional sub-blocks to fill in. I recommend that you start with the basic structure and then, when you are more experienced, have the ability to add further sub-themes to the text skeleton.

Introduction

Theme 1
   Theme 1a
   Theme 1b

Theme 2
   Theme 2a
   Theme 2b

And so on.

Revision

When you have a text that is presentable and meaty enough, all the revision (or rewriting) comes into play.

Remember: the quality of the planning you put in place during the prewriting phase determines everything that comes after.

A fatal mistake

What's the most devastating mistake you could make?

Going to change the lineup: the moment we have a skeleton that works we should follow it 100%, avoiding changing it in the race.

This is why a lot of people start novels and don't finish them: because they change the lineup.

The structure I'm proposing is a highway without traffic lights: the moment you have the car well set, the gasoline inside and the structure strong and powerful, you can press the accelerator and go straight.

First you are going to fill in these blocks on a topic you have decided on and then you are going to make a correction to the draft, adding an introduction and a conclusion and refining the title.

When following these three steps, we must remember to include the most important concepts in the first introductory lines.

By having a clear structure from the beginning you can ideally go on forever without ever running the risk of going off topic.

7

The rewriting phase

At the end of the writing process is the revision phase, called rewriting.

It's the crucial time when we'll think back to our reader and double-check what we've written, refining it and preparing it for publication.

Boiled brain

Never trust what you read: your brain is boiled (you've been working on it for several hours, haven't you?) and is likely to play tricks on you. There is an English saying that renders very well this idea of "myopia" of the writer: "too close to see".

How to solve this myopia?

If you can, it is always better to have another person read the text aloud. Only then will you be able to tell if the text is working or not.

I personally do something a bit bizarre: I copy the text from Word and paste it on a site that automatically reads online texts (like this one: https://ttsreader.com/). I get on the couch and start listening carefully to the synthetic voice, looking for typos or conceptual errors.

If you really don't have a chance to have someone preview your article, I recommend resting your eyes for at least 12 hours. This break will allow you to "detach" from your text and judge it more objectively.

Fine tuning

Then you go to make the fine tuning, trying to remove repetitions and refine the vocabulary, always taking into account the target audience and the mode of use.

Check paragraphs, idioms, phrases, words, nouns, verbs, adjectives… Review especially the beginning and the end, because these are the parts of the text that are usually remembered the most.

Set limits

It can be helpful to give yourself a time limit for each of these stages of ideation and writing.

The rewriting phase can't take weeks. For example, I normally spend a half hour on the creative and outline phase, an hour on free writing, and then at least a half hour on the revision phase.

These are the average times of an experienced writer: at the beginning it is absolutely normal to devote much more time to the three phases!

In conclusion, remember that you must always keep in mind all aspects related to Search Engine Optimization, the optimization of articles for search engines, so you can make your articles more accessible and more visible online.

8

The stated aim of your article

Every article has different goals, so always keep in mind what the purpose of a text is.

Always ask yourself: why am I writing this article?

Inform, educate, entertain

I love to take this adage from the early RAI broadcasts, where each of the three channels had a different purpose and audience. Remember that your article should always (and I mean always) have at least one of these three purposes.

If you find that it does not respond to at least one of these three goals, you are probably faced with an article that will interest no one or, even worse, an article of a purely advertising nature.

Expectations

Structure, as well as content, also communicates something to your reader.

The structure of the text has a kind of inherent rhetoric that anticipates to the reader what our real intent is.

You must always ensure an internal logic in what you write: you can do this by putting your hand to the actual structure and paying close attention to where you place the main argument.

Going to scan the structure of a text you are going to create in fact a horizon of expectations.

To better explain this concept we can use the example of cinema: if we see a trailer with sirens, chases and helicopters we will understand from the first seconds that it is not a western movie, but an action movie.

Thus, the structure of your text will also communicate the type of article, foreshadowing a reference genre to your reader.

Journalistic Format

We know that, for example, the classic newspaper article immediately responds in the first paragraph to the five W's of journalism: who, what, when, where, why and how.

The moment the reader finds himself in front of a structure of this type, he knows that he is not reading an essay, but a newspaper article that follows a precise format.

9

Finding inspiration with SWOT analysis

Looking for ideas

Let's move on to a very interesting topic: how to find ideas for your articles.

Clearly, there are many methods for finding ideas: we will look at some that can certainly help you get that cue, that creative launch from which to start (which in my experience I have found to be a real Achilles' heel of novice writers).

The editor assigns us a theme: how do we develop it?

The first technique I propose is called a SWOT analysis.

The SWOT analysis is a matrix: to make it, I suggest you take a sheet of paper and divide it into four parts.

Then write S for strengths, W for weaknesses, O for opportunities and T for threats.

You will then get four quadrants where you write strengths, weaknesses, opportunities and threats.

About what?

The topic you want to cover.

You can start by jotting down ideas about, for example, an event or a product and go on to elaborate on the strengths, weaknesses, opportunities it may bring and external threats (e.g. market, or environmental).

You don't have to use all of them, this process only serves in the creative phase to try to get some sort of focus on the topic and come up with ideas.

SWOT analysis was basically born for use on the product, but it can be applied to anything and can already be a start, a first cue to start making a list of topics to be covered in your article.

10

The "brainstorm"

Creative methodologies

There is another very interesting technique that I have had my students do in the classroom for many years always getting great results. It is a very fun methodology.

I'm talking about brainstorming, which is a creative method that I borrowed from my long experience in advertising agencies but that can also be applied to creative contexts in copywriting and writing.

How did I brainstorm in the classroom?

Normally I would work with classes of about ten students and decide on the topic of the article. Very pompously I would state:

"today our editor asked us to write an article about the well-known singer Vasco Rossi. Let's get to work!"

The students were all around a large table, positioned in a horseshoe.

First, I would do my best to write the word "Vasco Rossi" in the center of the board and circle it with the red marker.

Starting with the first student, in turn, each boy had to say a word that came to mind while imagining Vasco Rossi. Without thinking too much about it, because they only had five seconds before they lost their turn and passed it on to the next student.

A first level of consciousness

We would do two rounds like this, and the words I frantically wrote on the board (in random placements) represented a first level of consciousness.

Alba Chiara, music, concerts, disco … all rather obvious concepts, but still functional to our goal: finding ideas.

From the third round onwards, however, the focus was lost, people had nothing more to say about Vasco Rossi. Normal, isn't it?

And here comes the fun part. I advised people to start referring no longer to Vasco Rossi, but to the word the previous student had said. Always in a loose and free manner.

A deeper level of consciousness

The focus was no longer on Vasco but on the word that the previous student had suggested: guitar, melody, music, fun, being in company, having a drink, cocktail, beach, sea and so on.

The blackboard was populated, minute by minute, with a rich set of 50 to 100 words: an infinite range of themes to be elaborated.

We had brainstormed half Vasco Rossi-related and half free-wheeling.

Finding meaning

The thing I loved to do, the funniest and most surreal part, was to go to the blackboard and select five words with my eyes closed (five: does this number mean anything to you?).

You could always find a meaning in the chaos, which shows how the brain is inclined to find a meaning even where there is no meaning.

Maybe the key words I would circle were concert, drugs, being in company, work and loneliness.

With these key words I would suggest that students write an article "about Vasco Rossi's loneliness, in a period in which he had been particularly lonely, in which things weren't going well because he wasn't doing concerts (he was therefore out of work) and he had consequently fallen back into drugs, only to come out of it thanks to the company of his usual friends".

I highly recommend this exercise because it works excellently even if you are alone.

Do a couple of rounds, write about twenty words related to the main topic and then two or three more rounds trying to make a stream of consciousness (no longer focusing on the word in the middle, but on the last word you wrote).

The moment you have this word cloud, this cloud of keywords and topics, all you have to do is connect the dots to come up with great ideas for writing an article right away.

In this exercise I noticed that the hardest thing is to let go, to get into a connection that is fluid.

The moment you are not ashamed (if you are in a group) to say nonsense words you will discover how the most beautiful articles are born from these atypical connections.

If you are on your own don't fear your own judgment, with this method you can really start generating amazing ideas for your texts.

11

Mind maps

Another good example of a creative process for finding (and scaling) topics to pore over in our articles are mind maps, also known in English as mind maps.

How to make a mind map

To make a mind map you will need a sheet of paper and some markers.

Start, as always, by writing the key topic you want to talk about in the center of the paper.

From this core you will draw five branches, which will represent the five potential topics you want to talk about in the article.

These five topics may in turn have secondary branches that relate to them (as we saw earlier).

For convenience, I tend to keep the branches even: if I have two subtopics for branch one, I'll try to have two for the others as well.

What do these branches represent?

It's very simple, they will be the topics (primary branch) and sub-topics (secondary branch) of our article.

In this way we will have creatively created an outline from a mind map.

12

The BLOT structure

In the pages to follow, we will learn how to consistently and effectively structure our articles.

After learning how to find inspiration, how to determine the goal, and the three stages of the writing process, it's time to get down to the general scaffolding.

Let's keep in mind that, for simplicity's sake, we'll reason about the placement of key information. When to place them right away? When at the end? When in the middle?

The proposed structures clearly represent only a starting point and are of general value, but I am sure you will discover very useful information that will make you see the writing profession with different eyes.

Informing with the "inverted pyramid"

The most commonly used structure online is the BLOT structure, bottom line on top.

In the initial part the main information is positioned: title, subtitle, summary, who, what, how, when, where, why.

Think about it: at a first glance the reader will have collected a myriad of information.

Next, in order of relevance, we'll insert additional information: first paragraph, captions, summaries and other information.

By relying on this structure, the user will be able to understand the meaning of the entire article from the very first lines.

It is true that some readers read only the title, often made so that people click on it: we are talking here about the famous clickbaiting.

When you make headlines, avoid these techniques because in the end they are counterproductive as well as unfair.

Try instead to make the reader imagine, to empathize and to put in the first lines all the information that the user cares about, using emotional triggers that can fascinate and make the reader proceed in the reading (for example, in the first paragraph I often use "imagine that" to help the reader to enter an imaginative context).

One final note:

Rather than adding, always go in and take something away.

Your text is finished not when you have added everything that could be added, but when you have removed everything that could be removed.

13

The BLOB structure

You can make use of three types of standard structures when writing an article.

You are free to go and modify these scaffolds, but knowing them will allow you to understand how the highest systems of writing work.

Regular pyramid structure

One particularly popular structure is the regular pyramid structure, referred to as BLOB (bottom line on bottom). This is a structure in which the conclusion and all the main information is placed at the end of the article.

If the objective is to convince someone of the validity of our ideas, we will have to elaborate an argumentative text and therefore go to:

1. introduce the issue
2. develop the details
3. come to a conclusion

A text of this type will have a BLOB structure: the ideal scheme to promote, motivate, sell and convince.

In this straight pyramid structure, we will place the conclusions (the gist, the focus) at the end of the article.

14

The BLIM structure

Then we have the BLIM structure, bottom line in the middle, in which the main message is placed in the middle.

A text with a structure of this type presents the "conclusion" in the middle, and is the ideal scheme to give bad news or when we know that the message is unpalatable to our reader.

The "sandwich" structure

It is also called "sandwich structure" and is also used a lot in newsletters and email communications.

How to structure a text based on the BLIM structure?

A gentle and polite beginning, the actual news and a reconciling ending.

Anglo-Saxons talk about the three K's structure: kiss, kick and kiss.

A very common example can be when you apply for a position and the interview doesn't go well: often the structure of the email you receive is just that.

15

The tone of voice

A separate chapter is dedicated to finding the right tone of voice, the tone of voice, which represents the way you approach your audience linguistically, for example in your blog.

As human beings we can in fact "play" a large number of linguistic keyboards precisely because we are able to communicate through different registers: from the informal one that we use on Saturday night with friends, to the formal one that we may decide to use at a job interview (and all the nuances between one extreme and the other).

The vocabulary and syntactic structures we use change depending on our reader.

You should therefore ask yourself, "What register should I use to speak the same language as my audience?"

The target reader

If I represent a firm of lawyers and that firm has a blog, for example, I would avoid calling readers "you" and would push myself to use fairly technical vocabulary because the target reader might be identified in other lawyers looking for useful information (and familiar with the technical jargon, the language I speak).

If, on the other hand, I run a blog about travel, I might use a more informal and direct tone of voice in anticipation of a larger, more diverse audience.

Truth and judgment lie somewhere in between: it's up to you to figure out how to use syntax and vocabulary as appropriate to best communicate with your audience, speak their language.

Communicative aberrations

If you don't get your tone right, you'll experience what is known as a "communicative aberration".

Let's take an extreme example.

> *You are in the waiting room to attend a selection interview. You have prepared to respond in a formal, technical manner. You have no intention of making a bad impression. You've studied*

the company's history and customers, and your whole body and communication are going in that direction: you exude seriousness.

Imagine that you are wearing a suit and tie and that you are ready, based on your previous experience, for the formality that this situation normally requires.

And here comes the recruiter, in a t-shirt and shorts, who introduces himself to you in a childish way, immediately putting his feet on the desk and being too friendly and direct with you.

Can you imagine the situation? Here, you are faced with a communicative aberration.

Communicative aberrations can occur in everyday life as well as in writing. When you notice that there is no mirroring, that something is missing or that, simply, there is something wrong, you are probably facing a phenomenon of this type.

People expect you to use certain language that should never be taken out of context (clearly in the previous example the one out of context was the recruiter!).

So, ask yourself, "What will be the way I communicate?"

To determine tone of voice, we need to know the tastes, customs and habits of our target audience.

Our style is born, grows and develops depending on what is the path each of us takes online.

But having clear ideas is important, especially when it comes to professional online communication plans.

16

The gift of synthesis

It is very difficult to be succinct, and everyone who loves to write will surely agree with me.

There is a beautiful quote by Mark Twain that makes the point perfectly:

> *"I wanted to write you a short letter, but I didn't have the time, so I'm writing you a long one."*

It's much easier for a copywriter to write a long one than to keep only the essentials.

Fear of the void

We are victims of the so-called horror vacui, the fear of a void that we tend to fill with words, paragraphs and chapters.

The good writer removes, skims, throws away until the core remains.

Hemingway also stated:

> "I must leave up only the tip of the iceberg; everything else can be eliminated. If I manage to leave up the tip of the iceberg, it means that all my concepts are condensed there".

Units of Measurement

One of the most important pieces of advice I can give you on this is to chop up your text and use paragraphs as your units of measure.

Four five lines each paragraph and then a nice "wrap," a line jump and another paragraph.

Another definitely useful tip is to go titular on paragraphs (intended as a set of uniform concepts). When someone goes to scan your article he can immediately understand in which evolutionary position of your text he is and he can also decide to read only the paragraph that interests him.

Definitely recommended is the use of bulleted and numbered lists, as they ensure a simpler and smoother understanding of the text.

17

Bulleted and numbered lists

Arousing visual attention

A bullet point arouses a lot of attention within the flow of words (and the numbered one even more so).

Always ask yourself, "Can I insert a bullet point here?"

If the answer is yes, insert it, always.

It gives the reader breathing room and is a great visual hook.

The power of rankings

By the way: have you ever wondered why when you get your hands on classic "The 10 Things That" articles you read it so gluttonously?

Simple: because you know there's an end and you want to see what the number 1, usually the most important position, is.

It's not for nothing that sports broadcasts showing the day's goals keep the summaries of Juventus, Inter and the most followed teams last. To keep the viewers glued to the screen.

This system also works for the music charts: in the days of MTV there was the "top ten" and I remember that we had to sit through the whole show to find out the winner of that week.

In this kind of articles the numbers are in reverse chronological order: you start from position number 10 to get to the first one.

The "ranking" is a strategy that always works very well.

18

Punctuation and formatting

One piece of advice that is always valid is to go and use a basic vocabulary.

Do not complicate your life with vocabulary, always use active sentences, avoid passive ones, avoid adverbs, phrases, metaphors and everything you would insert in a text for the printed paper with the aim of "lengthen the broth".

Obviously, it depends on what you are writing, but in general, if you want to make your article clearer and more readable to the greatest number of people, do not play the D'Annunzio or Petrarch of the situation.

Use short paragraphs, short sentences, short words, always.

Replace the comma with a period

Always ask yourself, "can this comma be replaced by a period"?

Because if it can't be replaced by a period that comma makes sense to exist, if it can be replaced by a period that comma shouldn't be there.

This makes it possible to have a faster and tighter text and above all to have pauses that make sense.

Let's face it: we all hate super long paragraphs full of subordinates.

Visual anchors

We've already mentioned visual anchors, which are those graphic elements that allow the user to visually understand our article and hook our text.

Normally, bold is the most important visual anchor.

You can highlight key concepts or even the first sentence of the paragraph in bold so as to indicate them as important.

Keep in mind that bold should never exceed 20-30% of your article, because otherwise everything becomes important and the moment everything is important, nothing is more important.

Make good use of it and try to go to highlight the most relevant words and concepts, while avoid putting boldface on entire paragraphs because it makes absolutely no sense.

Italics, on the other hand, are used a little less online, for titles of literary or artistic works, interview responses, sub-paragraphs, captions, quotes, or for some foreign word that has not yet entered the common language.

Formatting

Formatting (shaping, in fact) can really make the difference between an article that gets read and one that gets abandoned instantly. It still happens to me, from time to time, to find blogs that offer entire walls of text, without even a line item to pay for it.

The temptation to abandon is great and compelling.

That's when putting a white space makes the reader breathe, because it's the most powerful punctuation mark of all.

Putting the "wrap" multiplies the points of entry and attention and highlights what's important.

Hyperlinks

Finally, the whole linking part should also be taken into consideration.

Don't be afraid to expose yourself by linking to external resources as well as internal ones, for example by linking the most important keywords to other sites that broaden the informative concept.

Take a look at a Wikipedia page to understand how proper linking works and take this site as a cue.

PS: Remember that it is very important to get lots of links to your article, because it is one of the determining factors for the ranking of your website.

19

Style Matters

Your style is determined by multiple elements that, combined under one pen, make your writing recognizable.

Your experience counts, but it is also given by the grammatical choices, the words, the structures and the tone you use.

Always ask yourself if your style is correct and if it goes well with the content and with what you are going to propose. Ask yourself if it should represent a personal image or a corporate image. Ask yourself if your audience speaks that language, that language, if they appreciate that tone.

As we said before, to define the tone we have two main parameters.

There is formality, which corresponds to the professional tone, and there is informality, which corresponds to the personal tone.

The personal tone has short terms, an informal lexicon, very contracted forms, the use of "you" and is therefore accessible to all.

On the other hand, when we decide to use a professional tone, we should not be ashamed to use industry jargon and longer, more complex sentences.

Your style and your way of presenting yourself depends, as always, on your target audience and the people who are going to read you.

20

Working on titles

Whether it's a blog article, a landing page or a newsletter, there's always a string that can catch the reader's eye: this string is the title.

A title must by its very nature be as effective as possible: it must catch the reader's eye and attention in the midst of the welter that is online communication.

The goal is to capture the interest, so a good headline must be incisive.

Please note: a fantastic title must always be accompanied by a fantastic article.

Here are some tips that I can give you to create headlines that "catch".

Be helpful

Write headlines that help the people you want to reach.

If in the title you are able to explain that thanks to that article you solve a specific problem, most likely those who have that problem will be invited to click and read.

Aim at emotions

Another good strategy is to focus on emotions.

It's true that people are looking for information on the web, but it's also true that they need an authoritative source that can speak to their emotional side.

Your headline could benefit greatly from this point if you go and mix information with emotion.

Question forms

A classic copywriter's trick to get attention is to use the interrogative form.

If you include a question in the headline, you have a better chance that the headline and consequently the article will be enjoyed.

Do's and Don'ts

You can also use the "do and don't" rule, suggesting to the reader what to do and what not to do (to solve a problem he/she cares about).

An example : "How to increase your engagement in five simple steps" or "How to devastate your engagement in five simple steps".

The power of numbers

As we said a pillar of good online writing is to organize posts in substantial points, proposing all kinds of lists.

Inserting from the title of the numbers strengthens credibility and simplifies, on a subconscious level, the expectations of our reader. Because if we communicate that the advice we're going to give is five, we're giving a somewhat limiting piece of information that reassures the person reading that title.

It's not about two hundred tips, it's about five. So read it, it will take you very little time.

The numbers can be even larger, in case our communication goal is to inform the user in depth about a topic in which we are knowledgeable.

Here are some examples of headlines that make use of numbers:

"Four tools to improve your guitar playing skills"

or

"Five Solutions to Achieve Good Results as an Athlete"
    or even
        "Twelve tips for the amateur cyclist".

and so on.

Inspire your audience

We can also inspire our reader with our title, positioning ourselves as an authoritative reference point in that particular niche.

Make sure that your readers find guidance in your articles: show your intent also and above all through your titles.

Always try to be clear, inspire and show clearly what your mission is.

Fear leverage

There's another very powerful strategy (but one that I don't recommend you use) to get your audience hooked right from the title: the fear leverage technique.

We all have a strong connection to fear, and eliciting that emotion can be a very strong hook, perhaps even too strong, for the reader.

Would you click on a title like "Five Methods to Prevent Burglars from Breaking into Your Home"?

I'll be honest: I'd click on it right away, because it leverages a fairly widespread fear.

The Lever of Empathy

Much better to try to leverage empathy to create a special bond with the reader right from the title.

To empathize means to walk in the other person's shoes, it means to feel the emotions that your interlocutor feels.

If you know your audience well, you can use your ability to connect by communicating this simple concept, "Hey look I'm like you and I've made these mistakes."

Show the way

You can bring your experience and recount your successes right in your headline: "How I managed to reach 100,000 plays on Spotify in 30 days" is a headline that would grab the attention of a musician (like me!), or "Six tips to turn your blog into a money-making machine" would make any budding blogger's eyes glaze over.

When you can, show the way to someone who is similar to you and would like to replicate what your path is.

The thing I want to remind you of is that you must always be authentic.

Only with experience and lots of reading, online and offline, will you really be able to get into that field where the game is seriously played.

The copywriter is basically paid for this: he doesn't have to go by trial and error, but he has internalized the rules, he knows how they work, he has experimented and consequently he can come up with texts that can work.

Conclusions

Writing for the web is a topic that could be expanded upon endlessly: my goal was to give you the basics, and I think the topics we covered (how to structure text, how to come up with ideas, and how to go about refining it) can be useful to many of you.

Good luck with your career as a copywriter (or for that matter, even as just an online writing enthusiast) and I'll see you at the next book.